Spectacular Sports

BASEBALL

Statistical Questions and Measures

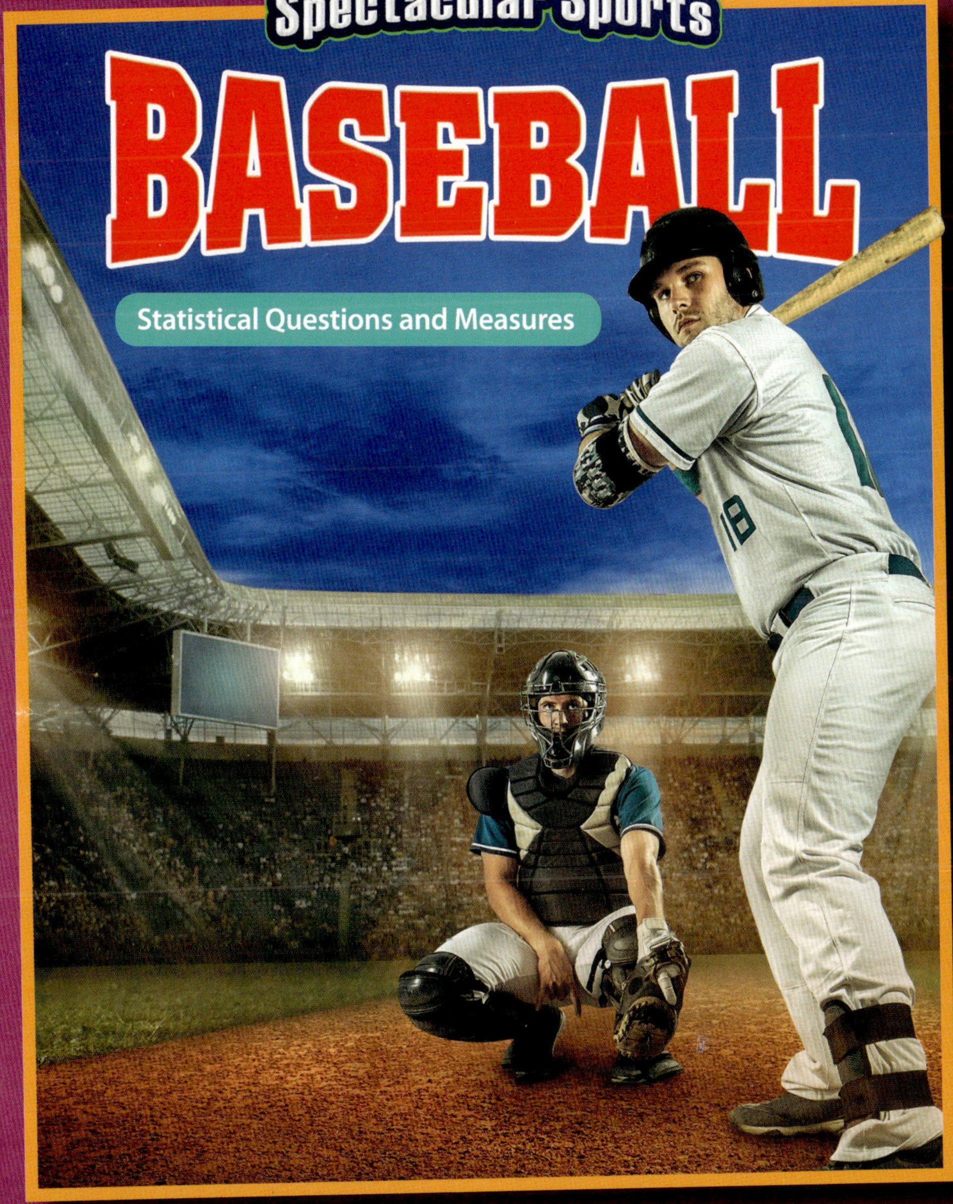

Marissa Hernandez

Contributing Author

Michelle Jovin, M.A.

Consultant

Colleen Pollitt, M.A.Ed.
Math Support Teacher
Howard County Public Schools

Publishing Credits

Rachelle Cracchiolo, M.S.Ed., *Publisher*
Conni Medina, M.A.Ed., *Editor in Chief*
Dona Herweck Rice, *Series Developer*
Emily R. Smith, M.A.Ed., *Series Developer*
Diana Kenney, M.A.Ed., NBCT, *Content Director*
Stacy Monsman, M.A., *Editor*
Michelle Jovin, M.A., *Associate Editor*
Fabiola Sepulveda, *Graphic Designer*

Image Credits: pp.2–3, pp.20–21 Joseph Sohm/Shutterstock; p.4 Keeton Gale/Shutterstock; p.5 Jenny Solomon/Shutterstock; p.6 (middle) Courtesy of the Hawaii State Archives [BL-2134-77]; p.6 (bottom) National Baseball Hall of Fame Library [BL-73.37]; p.7 Library of Congress [LC-DIG-ppmsca-18405]; p.8 Bentley Historical Library, University of Michigan; p.9 Library of Congress [LC-DIG-pga-04207]; p.10 (top) Mark Rucker/Transcendental Graphics/Getty Images; p.10 (bottom) Library of Congress [LC-L9-54-3566-O]; pp.12–13 Zimmytws/Dreamstime; p.13 (top) Eric Broder Van Dyke/Shutterstock; p.14 Pierre E. Debbas/Shutterstock; p.17 (top) Raymond Carlin III/USA TODAY Sports/Newscom; p.17 (bottom) Robert Hanashiro/USA TODAY Sports/Newscom; p.18 (left) Terry Schmitt/UPI/Newscom; p.18 (right) Valerie Shoaps/Cal Sport Media/Newscom; p.19 Paul Rutherford/USA TODAY Sports/Newscom; p.20 (middle) Sporting News Archive/Sporting News via Getty Images; p.21 (left, right) Courtesy Robin Erickson; p.21 (top) Francis P. Burke Collection; p.22 (bottom left) Erik Williams/USA TODAY Sports/Newscom; p.22 (bottom right) Meri Simon/KRT/Newscom; pp.24–25 Frank Romeo/Shutterstock; p.24 (bottom) Bettmann/Getty Images; p.26 (bottom) Ken Love/KRT/Newscom; p.27 (top) AP Photo/Darron Cummings; p.28 Library of Congress [DIG-ggbain-30907]; all other images from iStock and/or Shutterstock.

Library of Congress Cataloging-in-Publication Data

Names: Hernandez, Marissa, author.
Title: Baseball : statistical questions and measures / Marissa Hernandez.
Description: Huntington Beach, CA : Teacher Created Materials, 2019. | Series: Spectacular sports | Includes bibliographical references and index. | Audience: Grade 4 to 6. |
Identifiers: LCCN 2018051880 (print) | LCCN 2019005558 (ebook) | ISBN 9781425855376 (eBook) | ISBN 9781425858933 (pbk. : alk. paper)
Subjects: LCSH: Baseball--Juvenile literature. | Baseball--Statistics--Juvenile literature. | Statistics--Juvenile literature.
Classification: LCC GV867.5 (ebook) | LCC GV867.5 .H455 2019 (print) | DDC 796.357--dc23
LC record available at https://lccn.loc.gov/2018051880

Teacher Created Materials
5301 Oceanus Drive
Huntington Beach, CA 92649-1030
www.tcmpub.com

ISBN 978-1-4258-5893-3

Printed in Malaysia
Thumbprints.21254

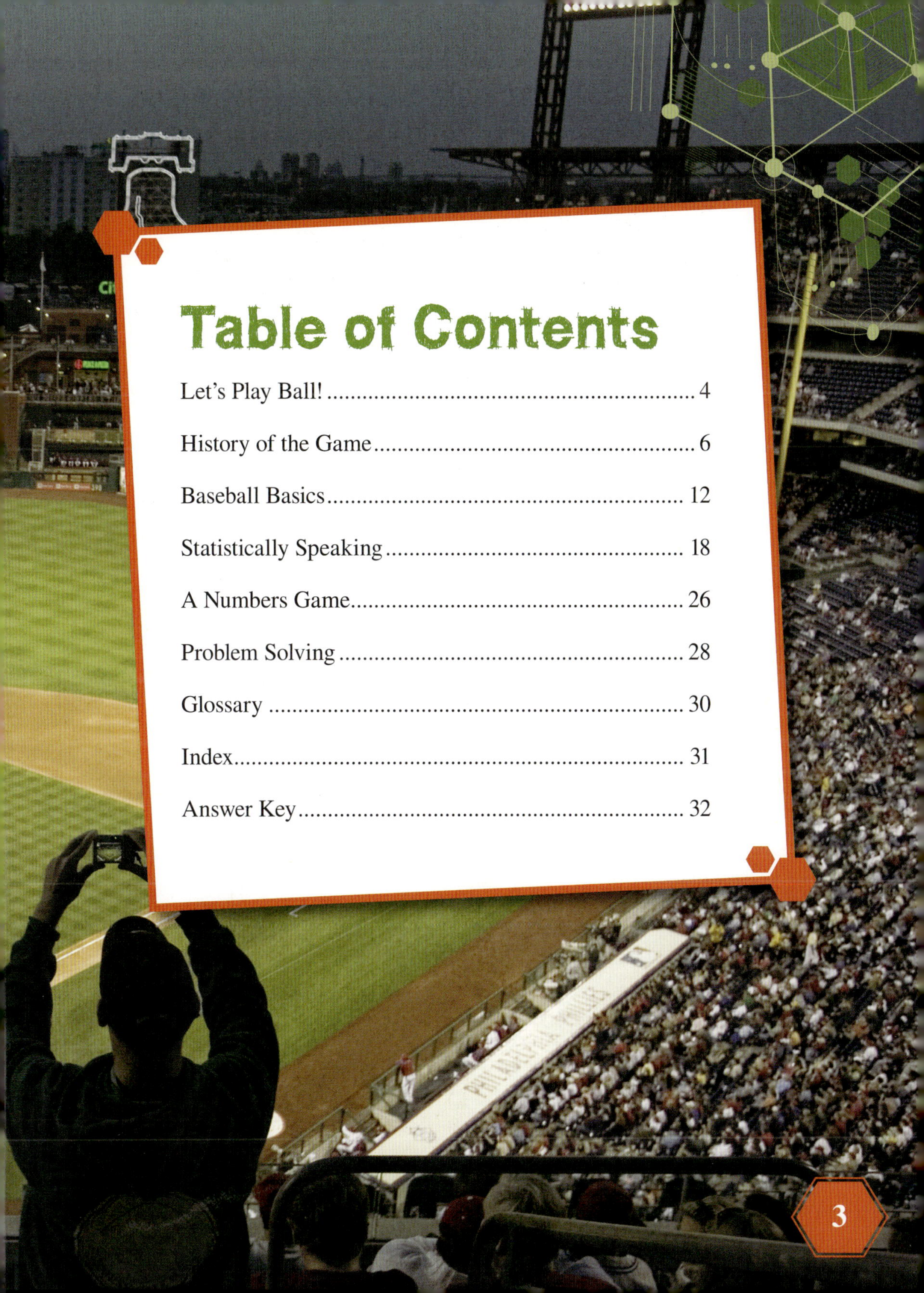

Table of Contents

Let's Play Ball!

One, two, three strikes…you're **out**! Baseball is known as the all-American **pastime**. It is also a numbers game. Every part of the sport involves numbers. Four bases, three outs, double plays, singles, no-hitters—there's no escaping numbers on the baseball field.

All those numbers add up to a game of **statistics**. Everyone, from players and coaches to analysts and fans, studies the stats. Go to a ball game, and you might hear fans discussing a certain pitcher's earned run average (ERA). A great batter will have **spectators** wondering just how high their batting average (BA) will go. And the scoreboard lists even more stats for people to keep track of.

In baseball, statistics make the difference between being the star of the game and sitting on the bench. Regardless of which team or player is your favorite, to truly understand and appreciate baseball, you have to look at the numbers. So, are you ready to step up to the plate?

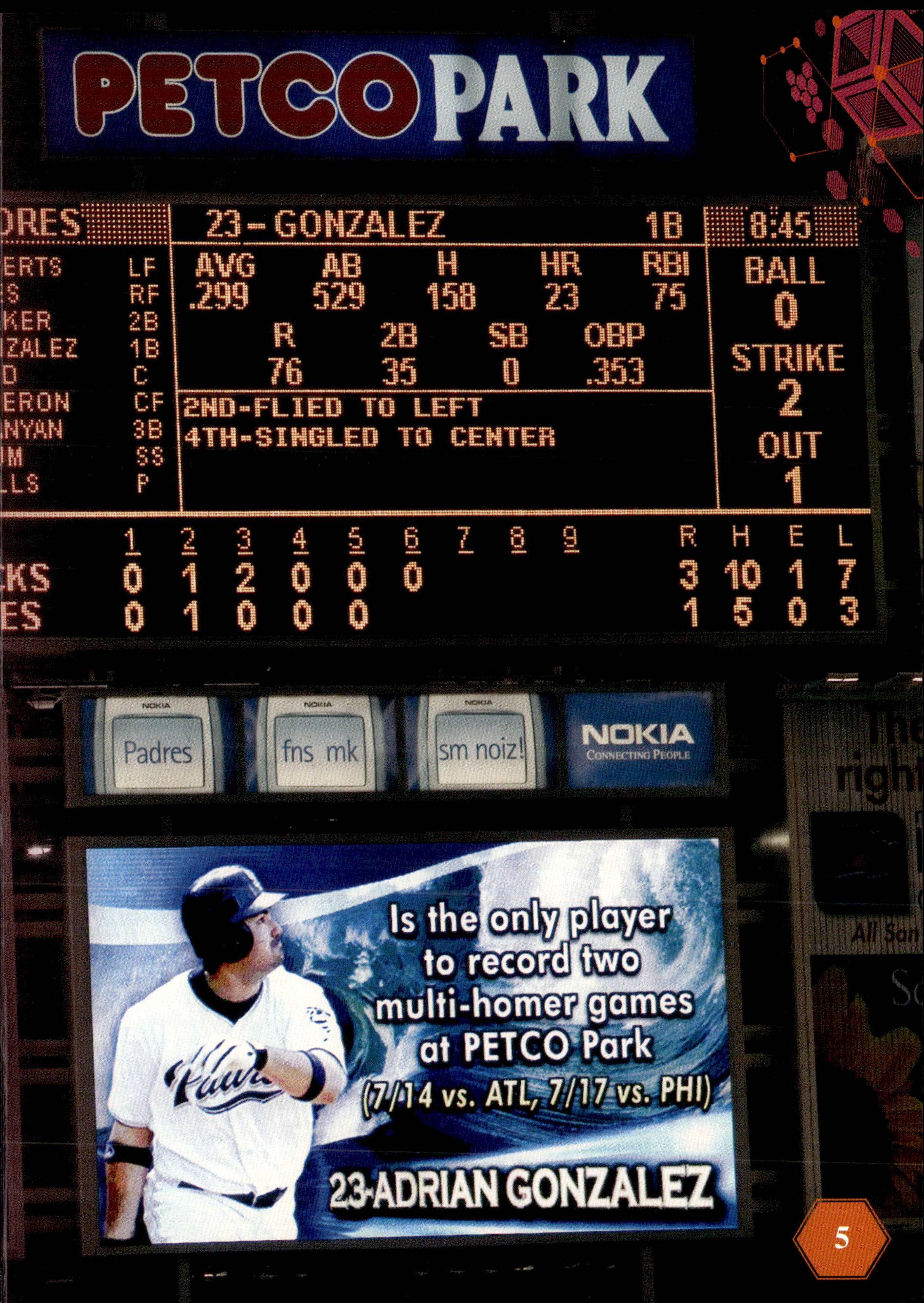
PETCO PARK
23-GONZALEZ 1B
8:45
AVG AB H HR RBI
.299 529 158 23 75
R 2B SB OBP
76 35 0 .353
2ND-FLIED TO LEFT
4TH-SINGLED TO CENTER
BALL 0
STRIKE 2
OUT 1
LF RF 2B 1B C CF 3B SS P
1 2 3 4 5 6 7 8 9 R H E L
0 1 2 0 0 0 3 10 1 7
0 1 0 0 0 1 5 0 3
NOKIA
Padres
NOKIA
fns mk
NOKIA
sm noiz!
NOKIA
CONNECTING PEOPLE
Is the only player
to record two
multi-homer games
at PETCO Park
(7/14 vs. ATL, 7/17 vs. PHI)
23-ADRIAN GONZALEZ

History of the Game

While baseball dates back to the 1700s, it didn't become popular until the mid-1840s. That is when a group of New York City men formed a team called the New York Knickerbocker Base Ball Club. A man named Alexander J. Cartwright was one of the players. He created a set of rules for the game, many of which still exist today. Baseball was initially played with a softer ball. That was necessary because the only way to call a runner out was to hit him with the ball! One of Cartwright's new rules was that a runner should be "tagged" with the ball instead of hit with it. The new rule led to a harder ball, which made games easier to play.

Soon, two types of baseball games emerged—the Massachusetts game (which still used the softer ball) and the New York game (which used the new, harder ball). Both versions of the game spread throughout the Northeast, with different cities choosing their style of play. Baseball was gaining popularity, but games were hard to play when teams from different areas played different styles. It took an unlikely event to thrust baseball into the spotlight. That event was the Civil War.

Alexander J. Cartwright

The 1859 New York Knickerbockers pose with the Brooklyn Excelsiors.

baseball poster from around 1895

LET'S EXPLORE MATH

In the 1800s, there were two different types of baseball games—Massachusetts and New York. Draw a T-chart, and sort the questions about the different versions. Then, write your own statistical and nonstatistical questions about this era of baseball.

1. Did fans prefer the New York or Massachusetts version?
2. Did the Hoboken, New Jersey, team play with a hard ball or soft ball?
3. How many teams played the Massachusetts version?
4. Which type of ball made it more likely for a player to get on base?

Statistical Questions	Nonstatistical Questions

Forming Leagues

As soldiers from the North joined together, they taught each other either the New York game or the Massachusetts game. The New York style was easier to play because soldiers simply had to find rocks to stand in as baseballs. By the end of the war, the New York game led the style of play. After the war, people moved west, taking baseball with them.

In 1869, the Cincinnati Red Stockings (later called the Cincinnati Reds) became the first professional team. Cities soon saw the appeal of having their own baseball teams. New **franchises** spread across the country. These new teams formed the National League of Professional Baseball Clubs in 1876. A few years later, the Western League was formed.

The two leagues played in harmony for the next few years. Then, the Western League asked to put teams in Baltimore and Washington, DC. The National League refused. The rejection angered the Western League teams. The Western League was renamed the American League, and the "baseball war" was on.

Moses Fleetwood Walker (third from right on bottom row) was the first African American to play major league baseball.

This print shows the players on the 1869 Cincinnati Red Stockings.

LET'S EXPLORE MATH

Decide whether the questions are statistical or nonstatistical. Then, write related statistical questions for the nonstatistical questions.

1. What was the first professional baseball team?
2. Which league had the most players in 1895?
3. What was the typical age of baseball players in the 1870s?
4. How many spectators attended the first professional baseball game?

Major League Baseball (MLB) was formed in 1903. That same year also saw the first World Series played between the two leagues. Fans loved the idea of the World Series—a set of games to see which league was the best. The series helped the MLB grow in popularity. When World War II began, baseball teams continued to play. The games provided a distraction from the horrors of the war.

Meanwhile, another league was attracting attention. In the early days of baseball, all men were welcome to play the game. But when professional teams began forming, most teams **discriminated** against black players. This led to the formation of all-black leagues. These leagues played alongside the MLB teams, although in much worse conditions. World War II caused many of these players to leave their teams to fight in the war. When they came back home, some baseball fans demanded **integration**. In 1947, Jackie Robinson broke the color barrier. He became the first black player to play modern professional baseball. After that, baseball was solidified as the all-American pastime.

Jackie Robinson was a member of the Brooklyn Dodgers.

LET'S EXPLORE MATH

A fan asks, "Of all the MLB teams who have won the World Series, what is the typical number of championships they have won?" Three sportscasters use the data in the table to answer the question.

- Manny says, "Typically, teams have won 1 World Series championship."
- John says, "Typically, teams have won 2 World Series championships."
- Barbara says, "Typically, teams have won about 4 World Series championships."

1. How can you tell which measure of center each sportscaster uses?
2. Which measure of center do you think is most appropriate to describe this data? Why?

Teams	Number of World Series Championships
New York Yankees	27
St. Louis Cardinals	11
Boston Red Sox	9
New York Giants	5
Philadelphia Athletics	5
Pittsburgh Pirates	5
Los Angeles Dodgers	5
Cincinnati Reds	5
Detroit Tigers	4
Oakland Athletics	4
Baltimore Orioles	3
Chicago Cubs	3
Chicago White Sox	3
San Francisco Giants	3

Teams	Number of World Series Championships
Cleveland Indians	2
Florida Marlins	2
Kansas City Royals	2
Minnesota Twins	2
New York Mets	2
Philadelphia Phillies	2
Toronto Blue Jays	2
Anaheim Angels	1
Arizona Diamondbacks	1
Atlanta Braves	1
Boston Braves	1
Brooklyn Dodgers	1
Houston Astros	1
Milwaukee Braves	1
Washington Senators	1

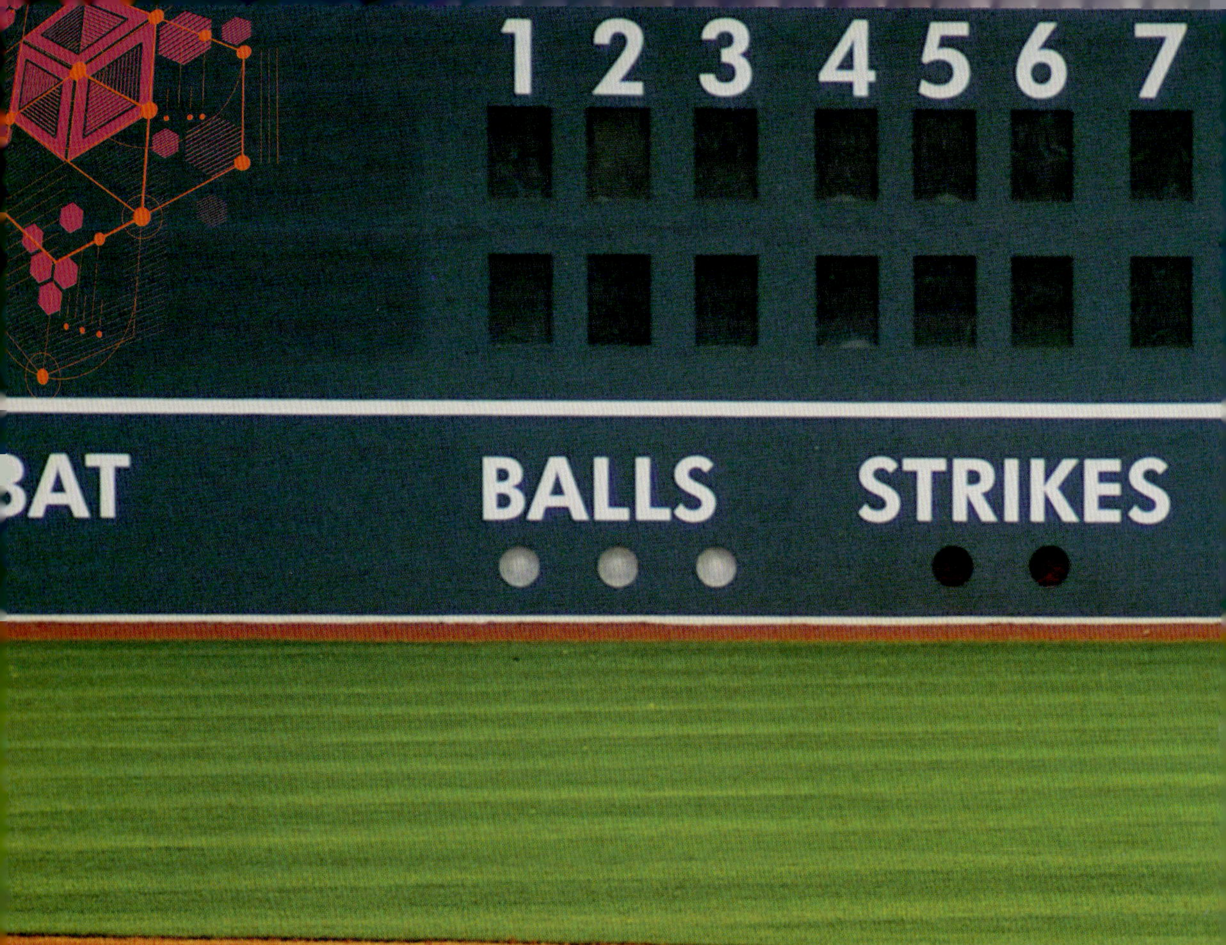

Baseball Basics

The point of a baseball game is for each team to score as many runs as they can. There are nine **innings** in a baseball game. The team with the most runs at the end of nine innings wins the game. If two teams are tied at the end of nine innings, the game goes into extra innings until one team scores enough runs to win the game. Sometimes, games can go on for hours. In fact, the longest game in MLB history was a whopping eight hours long!

Buster Posey waits for the pitch in Game 2 of the World Series in 2010.

Each inning lasts for three outs for each team. The team that is batting tries to score as many runs as possible before the inning ends, while the team that is on the field tries to stop those runs from scoring.

At the end of each regular season, the teams with the best records go to the playoffs. Eventually, the best team from each league plays each other in the World Series, the final showdown to determine the best team each season.

At its core, baseball is a simple sport, but fans know that their favorite pastime can get complicated quickly. There are many rules to follow and statistics to track, and to truly enjoy baseball, a fan must understand and appreciate both.

Get in Position

There are nine **defensive** players on the field at a time, including the pitcher, the catcher, and usually four infielders with three outfielders. Defensive play begins with the pitchers. Their goal is to throw a pitch that is difficult to hit. If they can get three strikes on a batter, the batter is out. Catchers crouch behind home plate and try to catch the pitches.

The rest of the players are there to stop the batters from getting on base. The infield is traditionally made up of four positions—a first, a second, and a third baseman, plus a shortstop, who stands in between second and third bases. There are also three outfielders who cover left, center, and right fields.

For the team on the **offensive** side, there are also nine players. These players try to score runs before the other team causes three outs. A team scores a run whenever a player goes around the bases and touches home plate.

The offense and defense set up at Yankee Stadium.

The defensive positions are numbered to help people record plays while keeping score.

Big Hits

There are many types of hits in baseball. Some names explain themselves: a *single* is when a batter reaches first base, a *double* is when a batter reaches second base, and a *triple* is when a batter reaches third base. A home run can happen in one of two ways. The first way is to hit a **fair ball** out of the park, which results in an automatic home run. Or, a batter can hit the ball and run around all the bases before the defense can tag him out.

LET'S EXPLORE MATH

A coach uses statistics to analyze her team's batting performance. She creates two dot plots to show how many singles and doubles players hit.

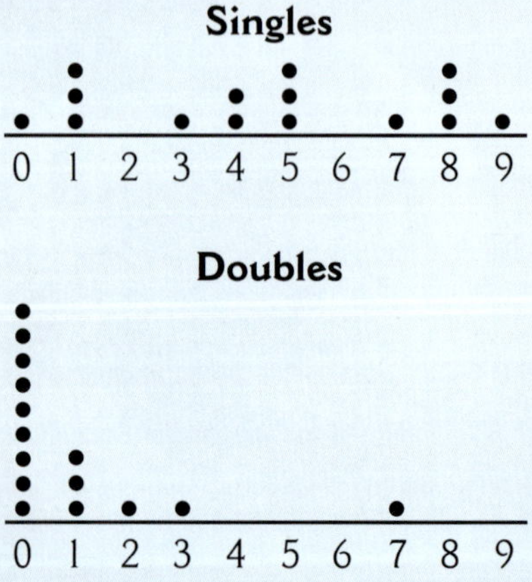

1. The range of singles is 9. The range of doubles is 7. What does this mean to the coach?
2. What is the median number of singles and doubles? Is this a measure of center or spread?
3. Describe the overall shape of the data for singles and doubles.
4. Do you think knowing the data's range, median, or shape is the most informative for the coach? Why?

Ryan Rua finishes hitting a home run.

The biggest hit in baseball is a grand slam. A grand slam is when a batter hits a home run when the "bases are loaded," which means there are runners on first, second, and third bases. A grand slam scores four runs and goes a long way toward helping a team win the game.

Baseball **managers** keep track of all the hits. They also watch their defensive players' stats to choose who will play. In baseball, statistics, more than anything else, determine a player's overall value.

Former manager Mike Scioscia watches his team from the dugout.

Statistically Speaking

Statistics are an essential part of baseball, especially for pitchers and batters. Everyone from the fans to the managers to the players themselves keep track of statistics. Take a look at some of the most talked-about statistics in baseball.

Pitch Perfect

One of the most referenced pitching stats is the *earned run average.* This number is the average number of runs a pitcher has given up over nine innings. For example, imagine a pitcher gives up one run in a nine-inning game. That pitcher's ERA would be 1.0. The lower the ERA a pitcher has, the better the pitcher is thought to be.

Depending on the type of pitcher, a coach may also look at other stats. Other key stats include wins, losses, saves, and strikeouts. The number of games a starting pitcher has won factors into how much playing time that pitcher gets. Relief pitchers have a different focus. They usually come into the game after the starting pitchers. For relief pitchers, saves and strikeouts are more important. All these stats help managers make decisions about the players they want on their teams.

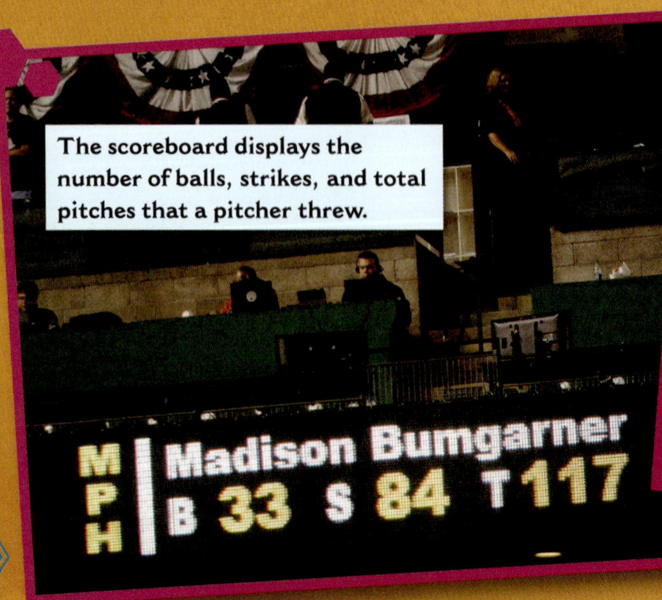

The scoreboard displays the number of balls, strikes, and total pitches that a pitcher threw.

LET'S EXPLORE MATH

Imagine that this table shows ERAs for pitchers in a community's baseball league. Different people use the data to draw conclusions. Decide whether each conclusion is correct, and explain why or why not.

1. The league commissioner says that the median ERA for pitchers is 7.
2. A local sportswriter uses this headline for a story: *The mean ERA for pitchers is 4.*
3. A team's manager tells players, "An ERA of 5 is common for pitchers in this league."

Pitcher	ERA
Aguirre	5
Deschamps	2
Flores	1
Jones	7
Murphy	5
Soto-Navarro	3
Zavilla	5

Masahiro Tanaka delivers a pitch in Fenway Park.

Managers and pitching coaches keep track of all these pitching statistics and more. Some stats are hard for pitchers to achieve and are rarely recorded. These include no-hitters and perfect games. Players who pitch either of these games have their names recorded in MLB history.

A no-hitter is exactly what it sounds like—a game during which a pitcher does not give up a hit. Batters may get on base by other means, such as **walks**, **passed balls**, or **errors**, but there are no hits. No-hitters are not very common; they happen about twice per season. Nolan Ryan holds the record for the most career no-hitters—seven! Ryan is also the record-holder for the most strikeouts. In his almost 30 years of pitching in the MLB, he struck out 5,714 batters.

This magazine cover from 1975 honored Nolan Ryan and his skill throwing fastballs.

Rarer than no-hitters are perfect games. Perfect games are when a team does not allow any of the other team's batters to get on base. This means there are no hits, walks, errors, passed balls, or any other ways for runners to get on base. Perfect games are very rare. In fact, only 23 pitchers in the history of the MLB have ever thrown a perfect game. And no pitcher has thrown more than one perfect game.

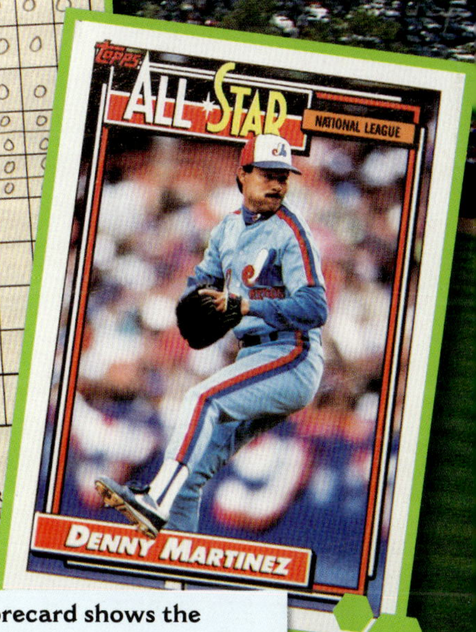

This scorecard shows the results of Dennis Martinez's perfect game on July 28, 1991.

Hey Batter, Batter

Batters also have many important stats to track. One popular stat is a player's *batting average*. This shows the number of hits divided by at bats as a decimal. Most MLB players' BAs are around .260. That means that they hit a fair ball and reach base safely (without the help of a fielder making an error) about one out of four times. Great batters have BAs above .300. You might hear a fan or sportscaster refer to this type of player as someone who is "batting three hundred."

Babe Ruth, shown here in 1921, holds the record for highest OPS.

Some fans think that a player's BA is not the best way to determine a player's worth. Instead, they claim that people should look at another stat—*on base plus slugging percentage* (OPS). This percentage shows how often a player gets on base, whether through hits, walks, or any other means. It also looks at a batter's *slugging percentage* (SLG). This number shows how many bases a player reaches per at bat. When those two percentages are combined, they show how often a player gets on base and how often they hit for power. For that reason, some people claim that OPS is the most accurate **assessment** of a batter's worth.

Jose Altuve, who had the highest BA for the 2017 season, hits a home run.

Broadcasters review the stats before calling a game in San Francisco.

LET'S EXPLORE MATH

The players on a school's baseball team are analyzing data about their batting averages. The players have questions for the coach. Respond to each question as if you are the coach of the team.

1. Ichino asks, "How can Reed's batting average be higher than mine? I have 2 more hits."
2. Shin is a new player who wants to improve. He asks, "How much separates my batting average from Reed's?"
3. Lopez asks, "Whose batting average is the median: mine or Martinez-Cruz's?"
4. Khadige is also the team's statistician. He wants to report the overall team batting average to the coach. He asks, "Which method should I use? I'm not sure if they are the same or different. Can you take a look at my ideas and give me your advice?"
   Method A: Divide total team hits by total team at bats.
   Method B: Calculate the mean of the 10 batting averages.

Player	At Bats	Hits	Batting Average
Reed	20	8	0.400
Hoier	22	8	0.364
Ichino	29	10	0.345
Khadige	16	5	0.313
Lopez	19	5	0.263
Martinez-Cruz	23	6	0.261
Nguyen	26	6	0.231
Ortiz-Lopez	9	2	0.222
Pham	23	5	0.217
Shin	18	3	0.167

Another important stat is a player's *runs batted in* (RBI), which tracks when a player contributes to a run being scored. RBI is a great measure of how useful batters are to helping their team score runs. Usually, RBIs happen when a batter gets a hit that scores one or more runs. Sometimes, this happens off a **base hit,** but it can also happen when a batter gets walked or even hits into an out.

Some of the most thrilling moments in a baseball game are when players hit home runs. They are another measure of a player's batting success. Home runs affect both batters' and pitchers' statistics.

Players who have hit many home runs are recognized. In the MLB, there are only three players who have hit more than seven hundred home runs in their careers. One of them is Babe Ruth, one of the best players in MLB history. He held the home run record for many years with 714 home runs total. Hank Aaron broke Ruth's record in 1974 and finished his MLB career with 755 home runs. Aaron held the record for 33 years until it was broken in 2007.

Hank Aaron holds up the ball from his 715th home run, which broke Ruth's record.

A scorekeeper tracks stats during a game.

A Numbers Game

People see baseball as many different things. Some see it as a game played around the world. It is the United States' national pastime and a favorite sport for many people. But first and foremost, baseball is a numbers game. There are numerous statistics used in baseball. Stats have everything to do with how the game is watched, how the game is played, and how the game is won.

There are many baseball professionals who study these numbers to predict winners and champions. These people are called *sabermetricians* (SAY-behr-meh-trih-shehns). It is their job to keep track of baseball statistics and to use those numbers to answer questions. If you want to be a sabermetrician, you need to work hard in math. Imagine a job that requires you to watch baseball all day!

Baseball is a fun and exciting sport. Whether it is rounding the bases, hitting balls, or pitching strikes, baseball players are always using math to be the best. So, with that said, let's play ball!

An employee enters statistics after a game in Cleveland, Ohio.

Problem Solving

Sportscasters often mention statistics when calling a game. They rely on teams of statisticians to give them the most important data. Imagine that you have an interview scheduled to work as a statistician for a sportscasting team. Before deciding whether to hire you, the interviewer gives you a project to complete to demonstrate your skills. Since Babe Ruth was one of the greatest home run hitters of all time, the interviewer is having you use his data. Use the requirements, histogram, and table to prepare your project.

Your project must meet the following requirements:

- Ask and answer a statistical question using the data.
- Calculate and describe measures of center, such as median and mean.
- Describe the spread of the data and what this meant in Ruth's career.
- Describe any trends in the data.
- Describe any outlying data points.

Season	Number of Home Runs
1915	4
1916	3
1917	2
1918	11
1919	29
1920	54
1921	59
1922	35
1923	41
1924	46
1925	25

Season	Number of Home Runs
1926	47
1927	60
1928	54
1929	46
1930	49
1931	46
1932	41
1933	34
1934	22
1935	6

Ruth's Home Runs

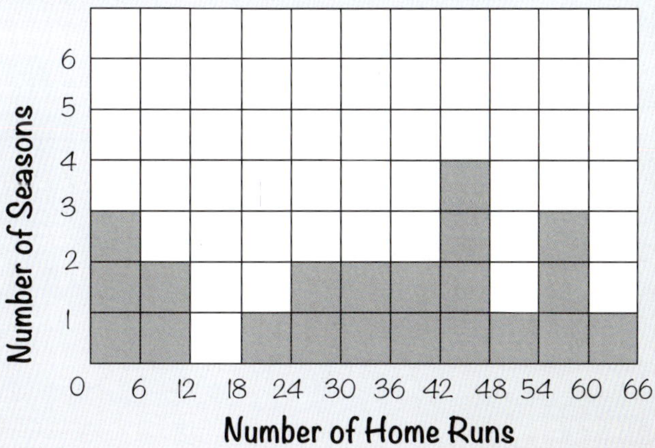

Glossary

assessment—the act of judging something and giving it a value or worth

base hit—a hit that allows a batter to get to a base safely

defensive—position in which players try to stop opponents from scoring

discriminated—treated a person or a group of people unfairly

errors—mistakes made by players that benefit the other team

fair ball—any hit that lands in the area between the foul lines and foul poles

franchises—teams that are members of professional sports leagues

innings—parts of a game in which both teams bat until three outs are made on each side

integration—the ending of a policy that keeps people of different races apart

managers—people who are in charge of the training and performance of sports teams

offensive—position in which players try to score against opponents

out—removed from play by the other team as a batter or a base runner

passed balls—pitches that the catcher can't control or hold

pastime—a hobby or activity that people enjoy doing in their free time

spectators—people who watch events as part of audiences

statistics—sets of numerical data that have been analyzed and generalized

walks—when pitchers throw four pitches that are called balls by the umpire, so batters are awarded first base

Index

Answer Key

Let's Explore Math

page 7

Statistical Questions: 1, 4; Nonstatistical Questions: 2, 3; Statistical questions' answers should vary, and nonstatistical questions should have one response.

page 9

1. nonstatistical; Example: *What were fans' favorite teams before 1900?*
2. nonstatistical; Example: *Did players prefer playing in the National League or Western League?*
3. statistical
4. nonstatistical; Example: *What was the average number of spectators for games in the 1880s?*

page 11

1. Manny: mode; John: median; Barbara: mean; Explanations may include calculations of mean, median, and mode.
2. Answers will vary. Example: *Median is the most appropriate because a few teams won many more championships and that data will influence the mean.*

page 16

1. 9 singles separate players with the most and least number of singles; 7 doubles separate players with the most and least number of doubles.
2. Singles: 5; Doubles: 0; center
3. Answers may include that data for singles are more evenly spread out, and data for doubles cluster left.
4. Answers will vary. Example: *Knowing the median is informative because the coach knows half the players hit more or hit fewer singles and doubles.*

page 19

1. incorrect; Order data from least to greatest to calculate median (5).
2. correct; $5 + 2 + 1 + 7 + 5 + 3 + 5 = 28$; $28 \div 7 = 4$
3. correct; The mode of the data is 5.

page 23

1. Reed has fewer at bats.
2. 0.233
3. neither; The median is 0.262.
4. different; Method A = 0.283 and Method B = 0.278; Method A gives more weight to players with more at bats, and Method B gives equal weight to all players.

Problem Solving

Projects must include statistical questions and answers, measures of center, and descriptions of spread, outliers, and trends.